SAFETY

by
Toni Webber

Illustrations by
Carole Vincer

THRESHOLD BOOKS

First published in Great Britain by
Threshold Books, The Kenilworth Press Limited,
661 Fulham Road, London SW6 5PZ

Typeset by Rapid Communications Ltd,
London WC1

Printed in England by Westway Offset

British Library Cataloguing in Publication Data
Webber, Toni
  Safety.
  1. Livestock : Horses. Riding. Safety measures
  I. Title II. Vincer, Carole
  636.1'4

ISBN 0-901366-89-7

CONTENTS

Introduction

Riding is a dangerous sport. Horses are big and strong, and even small ponies are bigger and stronger than their diminutive owners.

Ever since man first tamed the horse thousands of years ago, human beings have been the dominant factor in a partnership which depends for success on the obedience of one of the partners towards the other.

At times, this has been created by fear. Today, in most cases, the relationship is based on trust, and good riders work very hard to build up a mutual feeling of liking and confidence between themselves and their horses.

Accidents, however, can happen. When considering safety in relation to horses, there is no possible way in which to prevent the unexpected. The best that we can hope to do is to make the effects of an accident as harmless as possible.

This means doing our best to reduce the chances of an accident and to protect both rider and horse from serious injury should one happen.

In most cases, common sense is all that is needed to improve safety. Sometimes, modern technology has been used to reduce risk, and improvements in riding techniques are constantly being developed. Anyone concerned with horses should always be aware of the need to take care.

Rules and Liabilities

Legal regulations governing the use of horses are very few. There is a great deal of advice: from the recommendation in the Highway Code that horses should proceed on the same side of the road as traffic, to the suggestion that riders should wear hard hats at all times, but these are not compulsory. If you choose to ignore the advice, you may be foolish but you are not a criminal.

Nevertheless, riding organisations often have their own rules. No one may ride in a point-to-point, for example, without wearing a body-protector approved by the Jockey Club. And the Pony Club, which takes riding safety very seriously, has made it mandatory for competitors in all Pony Club competitions to wear either: a crash helmet that conforms to the British Standards Institute's BS4472; or a hard hat that conforms to the British Standards Institute's BS6473, kite-marked and bearing the following statement, 'This hat meets with the impact (or performance) requirements of BS4472.'

Legislation is quite strict with respect to the horse owner's liability for damage or injury caused by his or her horse. If your horse escapes from his field and creates havoc in a neighbour's garden, the law says it's your fault.

If your daughter's best friend falls off *your* pony and breaks her arm, you may be liable to compensate her for pain, discomfort and medical expenses. If your horse runs amok at a local show or plays up on the road and collides with a car, you could have a law suit brought against you for damages.

It is no defence in law to say that you did not know the regulations or that it was not your fault. Sensible horse owners take out insurance to cover them for personal liability.

Clothing

For many years, this was the kind of **hat** worn for protection by countless riders. It looked smart but it did not protect the temples and could break in a bad fall.

The **skull cap** was worn for 'dangerous' riding such as eventing. Its looks were improved by the silk cover. Now, it or the hat below are used for most events.

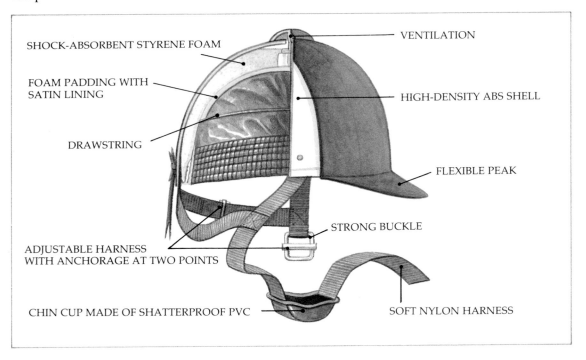

SHOCK-ABSORBENT STYRENE FOAM

FOAM PADDING WITH SATIN LINING

DRAWSTRING

ADJUSTABLE HARNESS WITH ANCHORAGE AT TWO POINTS

CHIN CUP MADE OF SHATTERPROOF PVC

VENTILATION

HIGH-DENSITY ABS SHELL

FLEXIBLE PEAK

STRONG BUCKLE

SOFT NYLON HARNESS

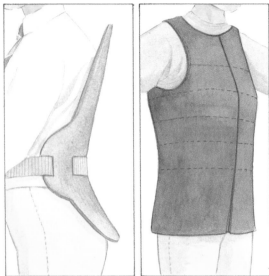

Two forms of **body-protector** in common use. Shaped, expanded polystyrene (*left*) protects the spine. Waistcoat type (*right*) guards spine and ribs.

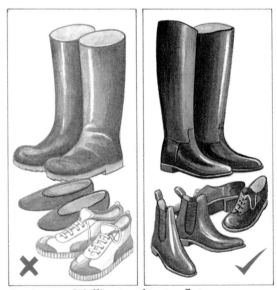

Footwear. Wellington boots, flat pumps and trainers (*left*) are unsafe. For comfort *and* safety, choose boots or jodhpur boots. Walking shoes with heels may be worn.

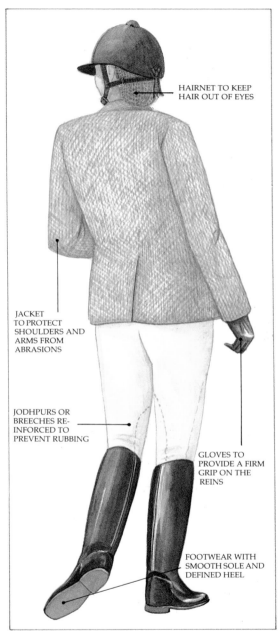

HAIRNET TO KEEP
HAIR OUT OF EYES

JACKET
TO PROTECT
SHOULDERS AND
ARMS FROM
ABRASIONS

JODHPURS OR
BREECHES RE-
INFORCED TO
PREVENT RUBBING

GLOVES TO
PROVIDE A FIRM
GRIP ON THE
REINS

FOOTWEAR WITH
SMOOTH SOLE AND
DEFINED HEEL

Riding **clothing** has evolved for safety and comfort. Modern materials are easy to keep clean and are smart in appearance. Many saddlers sell second-hand items.

Handling Horses

Common sense is a basic requirement when handling horses. The pictures here show situations in which carelessness could lead to accidents.

Horses have a wide lateral vision but cannot see an object close to and directly in front of them. For this reason, always approach a loose horse from an oblique angle. If you come up to him from the rear, he could lash out suddenly and injure you.

Ponies love root vegetables, but slice them into finger-shaped pieces so that there is no risk of choking. Offer a titbit on an open palm.

Never wrap a lead rope round your hand. If the horse pulls away suddenly you could damage your hand. When dealing with a pony's feet, crouch by him so that you can move quickly if necessary. When riding in company, concentrate on what you are doing.

Approaching a loose horse. Never come up to him from behind – he could lash out in fright. Walk towards him from an oblique angle so that he can see you.

A nervous horse can be **soothed** with a soft pat and a quiet word. If a horse is head shy, start with a hand on the neck and move it towards his ears, talking constantly.

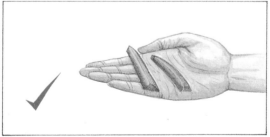

The right and wrong way of offering a **titbit**. Do not hold it in the fingers – you might get bitten. Slice carrots into finger-shapes and hold out on an open palm.

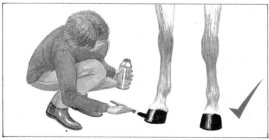

Lead a horse from the near side, with the right hand (as shown in the top picture) to give greater leverage. Never wrap the rope tightly round the hand for fear of injury.

Never sit or kneel when **handling a pony's feet**. You are at your most vulnerable in this position. If you crouch, you can jump out of reach should the pony move.

If riding in **single file**, make certain that you leave one horse's length between your own horse and the next. Crowding can lead to kicking and to possible injury.

Riders **in company** should never allow their concentration to lapse. However interesting your conversation, stay alert and keep contact with your horse's mouth.

Tack

Good quality, well-maintained tack is safe tack, so you should always buy the best that you can afford and then take the trouble to keep it in first-class condition. Never be tempted to cut corners by buying absurdly cheap new saddles and bridles – they are usually poorly constructed.

Stainless-steel bits and stirrup irons are costly, but they are better value than solid nickel, which is brittle. A bit which breaks while you are riding could have serious consequences.

Check the leatherwork, stitching, buckles and any parts where the leather is folded. Any faults should be remedied immediately.

Nylon webbing is an excellent material for bridles in daily use. It is strong and can be put in a washing machine. In wet weather, plaited or covered reins improve grip.

Safety and **standard stirrups. Rubber guards** give better grip and protect the tread. A stirrup that is the right size is about ¾ inch (2cm) wider than the boot.

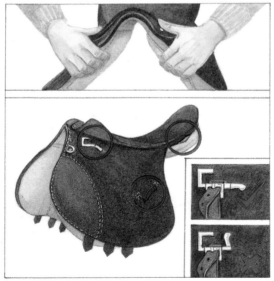

Keep an eye on the state of your saddle. Check the **tree** (*top*) by testing for 'give'. Red circles (*below*) show where **stitching** may fray. Keep **safety catches** down.

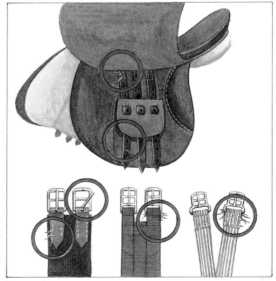

Watch for weak areas in the **saddle**, especially those under the flap. **Girths** are also vulnerable to wear, particularly the stitching and around the buckles.

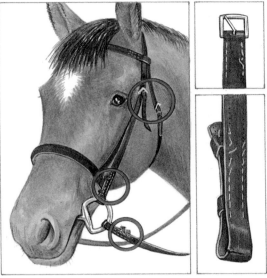

Weak points in the stitching on **bridles**. Check all parts of the bridle for damaged buckles and cracks in the leather. Carry out repairs at once.

For everyday use, a **webbing bridle** is hard-wearing. The parts usually fasten together with buckles, which can make it look clumsy, but it is strong, safe and durable.

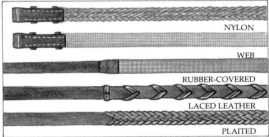

NYLON

WEB

RUBBER-COVERED

LACED LEATHER

PLAITED

Leather **headcollars** with brass buckles are very smart, but nylon webbing ones are ideal for everyday use. Tongued buckles are safer than looped ones.

Various types of **reins** are available which are designed to improve grip, particularly in the wet. **Rubber stops** (*top*) should always be used with a running martingale.

Road Safety

More riding accidents occur on the road than anywhere else, yet riders often ride two or three abreast, fail to give clear signals, canter on grass verges and forget all about keeping a sharp look-out for hazards.

If a horse is frightened, his natural instinct is to jump away from the object of his fear. Even the most traffic-proof pony may be startled by a bird in the hedge, and if he shies it will be *towards* the traffic. Good riders anticipate problems.

If there is ice about, ride without stirrups, crossing them over the pommel of your saddle. Let your pony keep his balance in his own way, and if he does fall you will be thrown clear.

Use reflective clothing or stirrup lights at dusk and in the dark, and put yourself between your pony and the traffic when leading him on the road.

Riding **at night**. Ensure you can be seen. Wear a reflective tabard yourself and fit leg bands on your pony. Best of all is a stirrup light, worn on the outside of the boot.

There are at least seven instances of **careless riding** in this picture, any of which could lead to an accident. Can you spot them? (See page 24 for answers.)

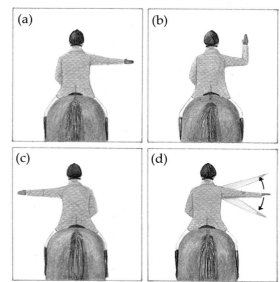

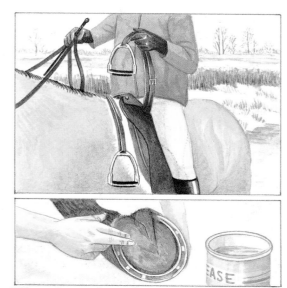

Hand signals given in the Highway Code:
(a) 'I am turning right.' (b) 'I am stopping.'
(c) 'I am turning left.' (d) 'I am slowing
down,' or (to drivers) 'Please slow down.'

When the roads are **icy** it is safer to ride
without stirrups. Cross them over your
saddle. To prevent snow from balling in
the feet, spread grease over the soles.

Travelling

One of the most enjoyable aspects of riding is taking part in competitions; more riders are buying trailers and travelling long distances to take part in the events which interest them.

You can still hack to some local shows, of course, but few organisers today provide horse lines where you can tie up your pony. If you intend to ride to a show, you should always allow plenty of time for the journey. If possible, arrange for a friend to take your equipment in a car. If you have to load everything on to your horse, put the bridle on over the headcollar and pack everything else into a rucksack. It is important to keep both hands free to control the horse.

Travelling by trailer is much easier and less tiring. Suitable travelling wear for the horse is shown below.

When buying a trailer, check that the floor, electrical equipment and towing bar are in good order and that the trailer is not too heavy for the towing vehicle.

If you are nervous about towing, try to borrow a toy Land Rover and trailer and practise manoeuvring them on the carpet at home. It will give you a good idea of how a trailer behaves. When out on the road, make all movements, such as slowing down and stopping, as smooth as possible.

Above all, never forget that you have a trailer behind you and that your vision is restricted. It is possible to buy extending side mirrors for your car which will give you a view of the traffic behind you. If the tailback behind you gets too long, pull into a lay-by and allow the queue to pass. Do not drive too fast. If the trailer starts to sway, reduce speed very gradually until the trailer stabilises.

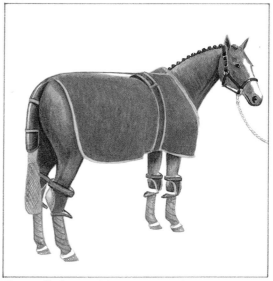

When **hacking** to a show, carrying such things as a headcollar and your lunch, it is important to keep your hands free. Put the halter under the bridle and use a rucksack.

The well-dressed horse ready for travelling. **Protective clothing** guards against injury. This pony wears rug, roller, tail guard, leg bandages, hock boots and knee caps.

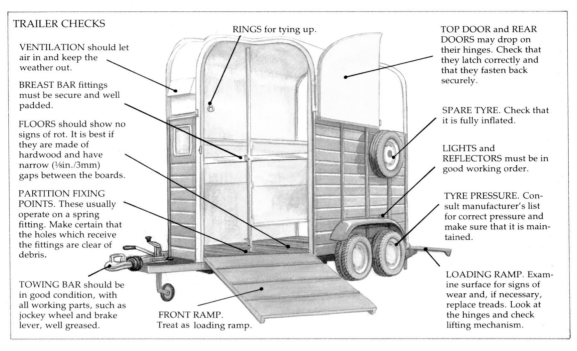

TRAILER CHECKS

RINGS for tying up.

VENTILATION should let air in and keep the weather out.

BREAST BAR fittings must be secure and well padded.

FLOORS should show no signs of rot. It is best if they are made of hardwood and have narrow (⅛in./3mm) gaps between the boards.

PARTITION FIXING POINTS. These usually operate on a spring fitting. Make certain that the holes which receive the fittings are clear of debris.

TOWING BAR should be in good condition, with all working parts, such as jockey wheel and brake lever, well greased.

FRONT RAMP. Treat as loading ramp.

TOP DOOR and REAR DOORS may drop on their hinges. Check that they latch correctly and that they fasten back securely.

SPARE TYRE. Check that it is fully inflated.

LIGHTS and REFLECTORS must be in good working order.

TYRE PRESSURE. Consult manufacturer's list for correct pressure and make sure that it is maintained.

LOADING RAMP. Examine surface for signs of wear and, if necessary, replace treads. Look at the hinges and check lifting mechanism.

When carrying one horse in a **double trailer**, travel him behind the driver for greater vehicle stability. Fasten breeching strap and shut front top door before moving off.

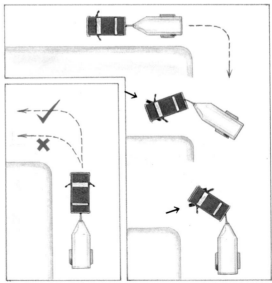

Manoeuvring a trailer. Do not cut corners. When reversing, turn the car wheels in the *opposite* direction from normal at the start, then follow the trailer once it moves off.

Tying up

Most horses accept being tied up quite happily, and they rarely make trouble. But even the most stolid pony can be startled into pulling back sharply or perhaps getting himself into a position where he could damage himself.

When tying up it is essential to use a quick-release knot so that the pony can be untied immediately if anything goes wrong (see picture right). The rope should be attached to a loop of string which will break or can be cut quickly.

Tethering should never be anything other than a short-term method of giving a horse a spell of fresh grazing. Always use a swivel post to prevent the pony from winding up the tethering rope, and make regular inspections while the pony is on the tether.

Never tie the pony to an insecure object such as a garden seat, a drainpipe or the bumper of a car.

Always use a **quick-release knot** (as shown above) when tying up your horse. Attach a loop of string to the tethering ring for extra safety.

A horse may have to be housed in a **stall** and **tied up** on a rope long enough to allow him to lie down. If he catches his leg in the rope, he could suffer a fatal injury.

For safety, pass the rope through the tethering ring and attach it to a **wooden ball** as shown here. The weight of the ball takes up dangerous slack in the rope.

Tethering gives a horse fresh grazing, but it must be correctly carried out, using a **swivel post**. This allows the pony to move around without getting tangled up.

Never use a **fixed object**, such as a tree, for tethering. Tethered ponies *must* be inspected regularly and should never be left on a permanent tether.

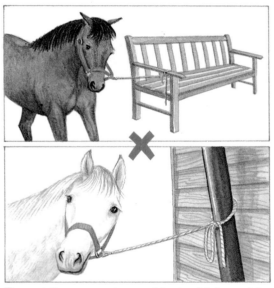

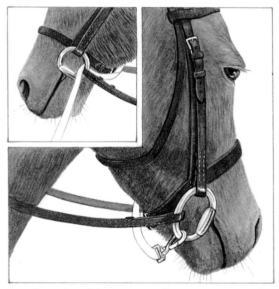

Do not tie a pony to an object which could easily break or move. Apart from the ensuing damage, the pony could be badly frightened or injured.

Leading should give you firm, *even* control over the led pony. With this in mind, always pass the **lead rope** through the near-side bit ring and attach it to the far side.

Safety in Competition

Walking a jumping course is not an excuse for chatting to friends. It is a vital opportunity for studying the obstacles that you will be tackling later and working out the best – and safest – route in keeping with your pony's capabilities.

At combination fences always check the distance between the elements. The fence pictured right, for example, can be tackled in one of three ways depending on the boldness of your horse and the length of his stride.

Check the terrain carefully and avoid areas with rabbit holes and roots. Make certain that jumps have clear ground lines. If you think a jump is unsafe, it is better to withdraw your entry.

Use protective clothing on your horse and sponge him down after your round, letting him cool down under a sweat sheet.

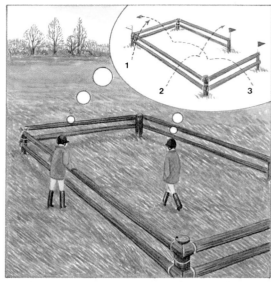

Work out the best line through a combination, and pace the distance accurately. This fence has three possible routes, each with white flags on the left, red on the right.

Examine the ground on both the approach and the landing side of a jump and plan to avoid rabbit holes and roots, even if it means taking the longer way round.

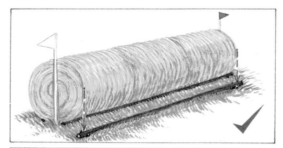

All jumps should have a clearly defined ground line and should never be jumped the wrong way. It would be unsafe to tackle the bottom jump from the left side.

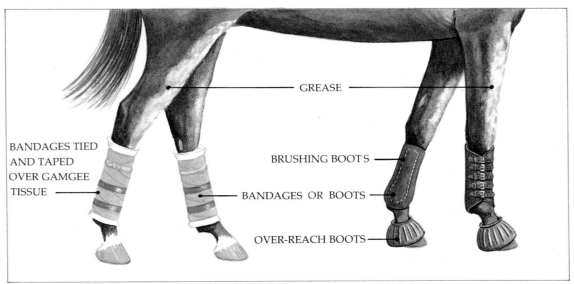

GREASE

BANDAGES TIED AND TAPED OVER GAMGEE TISSUE

BRUSHING BOOTS

BANDAGES OR BOOTS

OVER-REACH BOOTS

On a cross-country course, protect your horse with bandages, tied and taped, to support the tendons; brushing and over-reach boots to guard against injury to the front legs and heels; and grease, spread liberally over the front of the legs, to minimise the risk of injury should he hit himself against a fixed and solid fence.

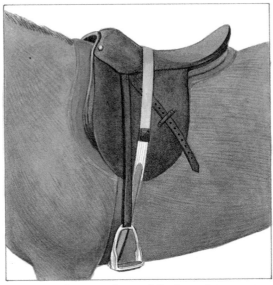

A **surcingle** over the saddle is an insurance against a broken girth. These girths have an elastic insert and are available in different sizes.

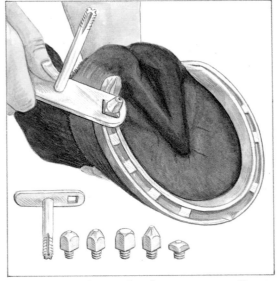

Studs screwed into the shoes prevent slipping. Ask your farrier to insert screw-holes into the shoes before shoeing. The tappet is used for clearing the thread.

Safety in the Field

The field should be one of the safest places for your horse, but it is up to you to make certain that there is absolutely nothing in it which could injure him in any way.

Fencing should be properly erected and readily visible to the pony. If you cannot afford complete post-and-rail, taut plain wire is an alternative, preferably used with a single top rail. The bottom strand should be not less than 18 inches (45cm) from the ground

Possible hazards, such as deep or stagnant ponds and poisonous shrubs, must be fenced off. It is particularly important to position the fence so that the pony cannot reach the shrubs and that dead leaves and branches cannot fall into the field.

If a public footpath borders the field, rubbish can get thrown over the fence. Check for and remove litter every day.

If possible, fence your fields with **post-and-rail** which can be seen easily and is very durable. Properly-stretched **plain wire** is adequate, with a single visible top rail.

Some **fencing** is very dangerous. Paling, sheep netting, broken rails and loose wire must be replaced. Never use a fence in which a horse could catch his foot.

Always check carefully in case **litter** has been thrown into the field. Look for broken bottles, old tins, and plastic bags, which can all cause injury.

Never give your pony **grass clippings**. They ferment quickly and can cause colic. If there are gardens next to your field, warn the neighbours not to feed your pony.

Fence off dangerous areas such as **poisonous plants**. Yew, privet, laburnum, laurel and oak trees heavy with acorns should all be well out of reach of horses and ponies.

A pond is a safe source of water if the bottom is of gravel, the approach firm, and if fed by a stream or spring. Stagnant, steep-edged ponds must be fenced.

An old bath used as a **water trough** is safe only if its taps are removed and the sharp edges boxed in with wooden panelling. Remember to clean it out regularly.

Safety in the Stable

The biggest hazard in the stable is fire, which makes it essential to ensure that the electrical supply is properly installed and that a strict ban on smoking is observed. Extinguishers should be suitable for dealing with fires caused by electrical appliances.

The second cause of stable-yard accidents is carelessness. Stable tools must always be put away after use and loose boxes kept free of clutter.

Artificial lighting is necessary in a stable but light fittings must be out of reach of an inquisitive horse. A standard bulkhead light should have an exterior switch. Plugs on all electrical equipment must be wired correctly and the socket outlet must have a protective cover.

Always make sure that the stable door is high enough and wide enough for a horse to pass through it safely.

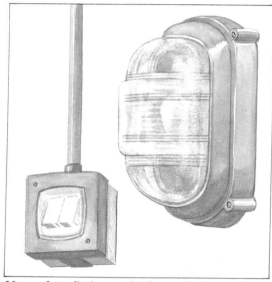

Use **safety fittings** which are designed for outdoor use and have weatherproof covers for the lights. A bulkhead fitting (*right*) gives ample illumination inside a stable.

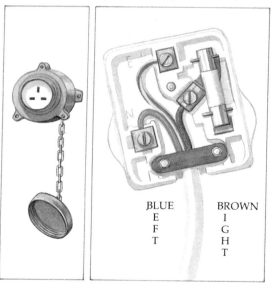

BLUE   BROWN
E   I
F   G
T   H
         T

Electricity is useful in the stable but can be dangerous unless it is correctly installed and wired correctly. Exterior power outlets should have safety covers.

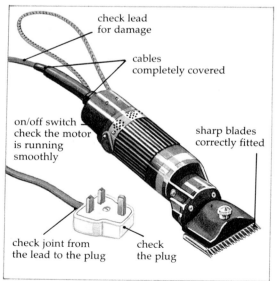

check lead for damage

cables completely covered

on/off switch check the motor is running smoothly

sharp blades correctly fitted

check joint from the lead to the plug

check the plug

If you use **electric clippers** make sure that they are earthed. Service them regularly, and clean them after use. Check the supply cable as well as the working parts.

Keep **stable fittings** to the minimum. A manger and haynet ring are quite adequate equipment. The water bucket may be put in an old tyre or mounted in a wall rack.

Ban smoking from the stable yard and install **fire extinguishers** in readily accessible places. Do not use the liquid type on an electrical fire. Label clearly.

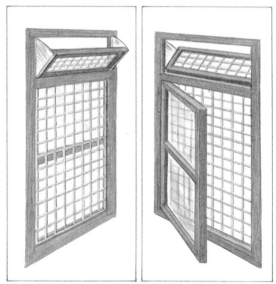

Cover **windows** with galvanised mesh. For ventilation, the best windows are the type that have a top vent opening inwards. This directs air upwards and prevents draughts.

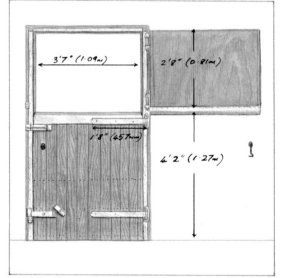

Stable doors can injure a horse, usually because they are too narrow and the animal bangs himself when passing through. These are the minimum dimensions.

Safety From Theft

Expensive tack is particularly vulnerable to thieves and sometimes horses and ponies are stolen. They can all be protected by indelible labelling. Freeze-marking is a painless process which permanently stamps a horse's number on his back, usually under the saddle. The number is held on a central register. Tack can be marked with a special pen. Padlocks and name tapes are mainly effective against casual crime.

What did you spot? (see page 12)
1. Riders three abreast.
2. Leading-rein rider on the outside.
3. Middle rider has no hat.
4. Inside pony's leg bandage coming undone.
5. Rider cantering on grass verge.
6. Dismounted rider leading from near side.
7. Stirrups left dangling.

In addition, hazards include milk churns, children playing, loose dog, potholes, pigs, muddy puddles, litter and hidden drains on the grass verge.

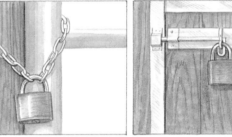

The best protection from horse thieves is provided by **freeze-marking** (*top*). Intruders are deterred by **padlocks** on gates and doors but be sure to keep the keys safe.

Mark equipment by using a special pen with writing that is invisible to the naked eye but shows up under ultraviolet rays. Sew **name tapes** on equipment.

Thieves can have four legs as well as two. Keep **feed bins** well away from horses, preferably in a shed with a door. A greedy horse could get a severe dose of colic.